Date: 1/21/22

BR 599.772 NIL
Nilsen, Genevieve,
Dingo pups /

TOOLS FOR CAREGIVERS

- **F&P LEVEL:** D
- **WORD COUNT:** 39

- **CURRICULUM CONNECTIONS:**
  animals, habitats

Skills to Teach

- **HIGH-FREQUENCY WORDS:** a, are, in, is, it, their, these, they
- **CONTENT WORDS:** born, called, den, dingo, drink, fur, group, grow, howl, live, milk, Mom's, pack, play, pups, run, tan
- **PUNCTUATION:** exclamation points, periods
- **WORD STUDY:** long /a/, spelled ay (play); long /o/, spelled ow (grow); /oo/, spelled oo (awoo); /ow/, spelled ow (howl); short /a/, spelled a (are, called, pack, tan)
- **TEXT TYPE:** factual description

Before Reading Activities

- Read the title and give a simple statement of the main idea.
- Have students "walk" through the book and talk about what they see in the pictures.
- Introduce new vocabulary by having students predict the first letter and locate the word in the text.
- Discuss any unfamiliar concepts that are in the text.

After Reading Activities

Ask readers to compare dingo pups and puppies. How are they similar? How are they different? If students struggle to come up with answers, flip back through the book. Explain to readers that both dingo pups and puppies are born with siblings. Both drink milk from their mothers. They also run and play. Ask readers to note their physical similarities and differences.

Tadpole Books are published by Jump!, 5357 Penn Avenue South, Minneapolis, MN 55419, www.jumplibrary.com

Copyright ©2022 Jump. International copyright reserved in all countries. No part of this book may be reproduced in any form without written permission from the publisher.

Editor: Jenna Gleisner **Designer:** Molly Ballanger

Photo Credits: Nicole Patience/iStock, cover, 2bl, 8–9; ozflash/iStock, 1; Jean-Paul Ferrero/Pantheon/SuperStock, 2tl, 2br, 3, 4–5; slowmotiongli/Shutterstock, 6–7; CraigRJD/iStock, 2tr, 2ml, 10–11, 14–15; Imagebroker/Alamy, 2mr, 12–13; Andrew Haysom/iStock, 16.

Library of Congress Cataloging-in-Publication Data
Names: Nilsen, Genevieve, author.
Title: Dingo pups / by Genevieve Nilsen.
Description: Minneapolis: Jump!, Inc., 2022. | Series: Outback babies | Includes index. | Audience: Ages 3–6
Identifiers: LCCN 2020046241 (print) | LCCN 2020046242 (ebook) | ISBN 9781645279402 (hardcover)
ISBN 9781645279419 (paperback) | ISBN 9781645279426 (ebook)
Subjects: LCSH: Dingo—Infancy—Juvenile literature.
Classification: LCC QL737.C22 N557 2022 (print) | LCC QL737.C22 (ebook) | DDC 599.77/21392—dc23
LC record available at https://lccn.loc.gov/2020046241
LC ebook record available at https://lccn.loc.gov/2020046242

OUTBACK BABIES

DINGO PUPS

by Genevieve Nilsen

TABLE OF CONTENTS

WORDS TO KNOW

den

fur

howl

pack

play

pups

DINGO PUPS

pup

These are dingo pups!

mom

They are born in a den.

They drink Mom's milk.

They run.

They play!

9

They grow.

fur

Their fur is tan.

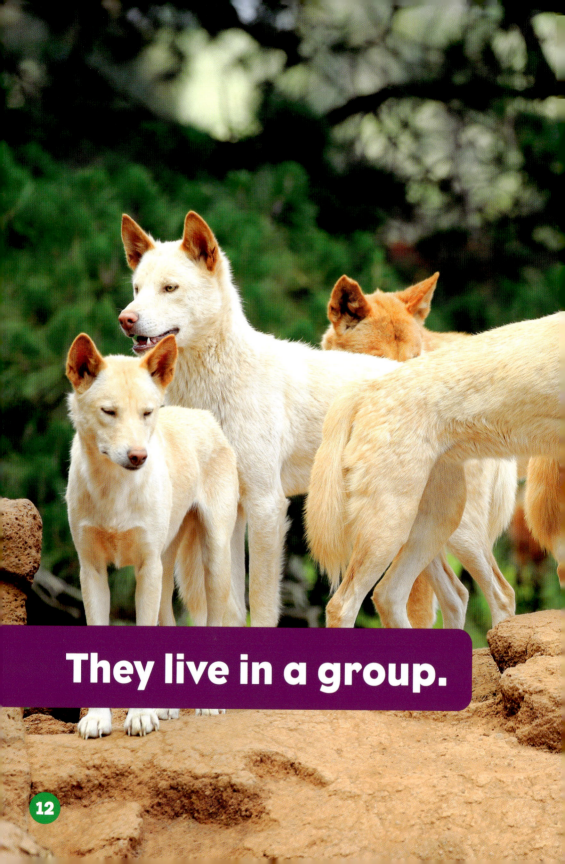

They live in a group.

pack

It is called a pack.

13

They howl.

Awoo!

LET'S REVIEW!

What are these dingo pups doing?

INDEX